THE BLUE MUSE

S.J. Lomas

8N PUBLISHING

THE BLUE MUSE

1st Edition published by 8N Publishing, LLC
P.O. Box 972364
Ypsilanti, MI 48197

Front cover design by Rock Solid Book Design, Book Covers by Mallory Rock

Also by S.J. Lomas

YA Novels:
Dream Girl
Dream Frequency

Short stories:
Kiss of Death
Sick Day

Keep abreast of new works at
www.sjlomas.com
Follow on Amazon, Goodreads, Facebook,
or Twitter @SJLomasAuthor

This collection is dedicated to:

Paul D. McGlynn, the most influential poetry and literature professor. You'll always be missed.

Saint Peter's College summer class of 1999.

Lang Leav, for writing such simple, yet exquisite, poetry.

A Surrealist's Saturday

For Paul McGlynn

Dripping.
Saturday drips down
Slides over the legs
Of our kitchen table.
Spilt milk falls faster
This is more like
Heated caramel.
Shall we wipe it clean,
Or let it collect in a pool?
Would it be okay
On a linoleum floor?
Sunday breezes will cool it off,
Make it solidify there.
Crusting lazily,
'Til you notice again.

Oblong Summer Day

The summer day floated around
in a typical oblong orbit.
Birds whistled Mendelssohn
in his most sopranic madness.
Trees expanded in nuclear clouds
of Monet light flecks and color.
The sun sent yellow heat
to optical illusionize the air and sky.
And I? I meandered past Victorian houses
on a dirt road because the day
invited me to enjoy.

Con Molta Passione!

A sonic wind flows through my hair
We road trip up the expressway together
The bass line pumps through the speakers,
Beating my heart for me.
Feet curved to fit on the trembling dashboard
Eyes close, lips curve Heavenward
Rhythm! Rhythm! Tears my soul from earthly shackles
Erupts in an orgasm of aural delight
No perception left as powerful as the audio
It sends my insides quivering
I'm shaking in its wake
Like an addict, I crave more.

An Evangeline

I came to you
Last Sunday
To snuggle in
your beauty.
Light orbitals
Silent from your lips.
Scent like ginger
Staring from your hair.
Loud rainbows
All over the floor.
You are such a sun
On my heart.
How did you rise there?
When must you set?
Your woodgrain of goodness.
So red to love you,
And yellow.

Rain Runner

My beautiful rain runner,
Why don't you wait?
Bowing your head to avoid drops
Is the wet so offensive you must scorn it?
Rushing toward shelter, craving the dry
While I stroll through puddles in common time
Hold open the door letting me pass
A convenient gentleman at times most sweet
To woo the princess that is me.
Wait to be seated at slimy restaurant table
Tacky songs clamor from the speaker above
Sticky plastic coated menu between lotiony fingers
Decide your palate for the evening
I'm not hungry, but I'll eat to be with you
Sometimes looking past you to rainy gusts tilting trees.
Both sipping our courtesy water
We sneak glances at each other
Taking a moment to reflect...
You say we're especially great together
Our connection is rare and strong
You speak these things.
You sip more water.
But alas, you see, we've missed our one chance
Couldn't wiggle through our pinhole of opportunity
We nod, twisting our mouths in wax smiles
Indeed, a terrible shame how our worlds turn.
But isn't that how life tends to go?
A whole life out the pinhole we couldn't squeeze through.
"But we're buddies, right? Special souls?"
"Of course, my friend, quite close."

Waiter bring the food
Mine very hot, yours slightly cold
Eat your meal, Dear, make yourself whole
Forget you'd said anything important at all.
But I'll remember the words you chose
I'll preserve the wistful regret of your eyes
Keep it hidden in some secret locket
Where it will sleep, in pure darkness, forever.

L'Anima d'Amore

Two ordinary people, simple man, simple woman
Share their attraction in the nighted woods
The Eternal Kiss, by poets immortalized,
Floats electrically across their moist lips
Pulse intensifies, passions rise
Moonlight love romanticizes all
The cliché symphonies of violin, flute, harp
Prove themselves to be true,
Not as strings on instruments plucked,
but as heartbeats, as sighs, purest joy
Who ever knew how a soul could dance,
Yet it knows the motions well:
Gliding like butterflies on midnight air
Soaring, breathing, twisting, twirling
Innocent loving, made true this night
Annointed by moonlight and earth.

The Gothic Gaze

Standing on a Grecian Column
Waving my arms at a star's light
A Gothic gaze glaring over the hills
At a moment past sunset.
Wind is blowing through my skirt,
Whipping my hair back...
Streaming for miles away.
I am of mythic proportions,
Reigning as the goddess of joy,
Crowned with laurels,
Wearing an olive twig round my neck,
Clasping a goblet of wine.
Dancing in sandals
As the sky grows dark.
No one else takes note of me,
I am up too high.
Seemingly solitary in the night
But surrounded by happiness of you
In my heart, in my thoughts...
Your taste still lingers on my lips
Your scent still clings to my skin.
Not abandoned and lost at all.
I cannot moan and cry
For one just over those hills.
Parting is never forever,
Not even at the end of time.
So I dance and embrace the starlight
While I rejoice in love's wonders myself.

Starship Melody

Music ascends like a spaceship
Maneuvering up and away
Whirring far from heavy life
Floating like sunbeams.
Sometimes, it clips itself with clothespins
To your heart, and pulls that up too.
Dancing and swaying,
Twirling and gliding with the stars.

The Un-season

Woven into the links of a silver promise,
a forbidden sonnet.
Crackling whispers and robed desires.
A bond without place and time to be.
A shaking tendril of one soul to another,
choked by a frostbitten flirtation
And a bootleg season of glances.
I flatten my soul into a banded mist-
Hoping to float on a breeze-
To be inhaled
So we may be contained together. For a time.
There is only one moment for miracles,
Blurred as a passing train.
Even though the sprout withers to brown,
The roots shall never die.
Hidden beneath the parched surface
The rusty, weathered elegance
Of the uncultivated song.

Blind Music of the Legendary Angel Discovered

What young aural poet
lets his seraphs fly in your soul?
Can he pull out dusty dreams,
long forgotten in your attic,
with one ethereal note from Heaven,
sounded precisely at the moment of destiny?
You look so perfect, as I see you,
from behind my morning dew of tears.
His moonlight voice shines silvering,
playing softly on your hair.
You thought Christine's Angel
was no more than crafted fancy,
yet I told you I would find him.
I always believed, didn't I?
Ascend with me,
the Golden Ear staircase to Heaven.
Close your misty eyes and follow blindly.
Eyes aren't needed for the soul to feel.
He's sung you to Paradise,
like the old promise read.
Couldn't be any closer
unless the soul were a violin.
Bless the bone and soul angels
who rare times travel earth.
Lead on, Music Spirit, sing to me forever.
I will follow you.
Rapture filled, I go.
Soaring from the holy mountain
of your ever sanctifying note.

Eight Nudes Dancing In Still Life

Born and baptized once and forever,
Humbled, the baby of nature
Writhing seaweed child in nondescript coolness
Loosing the anchor from the sand
Emerging to life with the seven sisters
In the circle of paleness and dark.
Sleek, and fast to the head
Is the angel hair of new life.
All faces turn to shooting stars
Whirling fast past other diamonds of Heaven
Be free, my child, come Be with us
Let baptism polish your soul
Your sisters are connected to you
Feel it in the calm heaviness that surrounds you
Let go, let go. Sigh deep. It floats away.
Where do I end and the life force begin?
The stars tell me it matters little
For I am my sisters
And they are the ocean
And this will be our home.

Rainstorm

Dust, like billowing smoke, rises in the wind.
Sun is out, distorted in the haze.
Cicadas emit their distinctive Zzzzzz,
in the oppressive, motionless heat.
Life is still. Rests in a pleading ritual.
Waiting languidly for rain.
Not even the breeze invigorates.
Only refreshing as an oven to a baking cake.
And there's waiting...
Such stifling waiting.
And watching as life dries up.
Like me.
Me without you.
There is no crackling thunderstorm
to dance in during the night.
Only shimmering mirages on the blacktop
of heat puddles to splash our shoes in.
I can only check my watch, waiting for the winds to change
and bring the pregnant clouds to my home.
Washing the stones. Rushing water down the sidewalk.
Bringing salvation to this barren lifelessness.
Offering energy and sweetness again.

The Blue Muse

She steals in at night.
Languid curves in draping silk,
backlit by lightning and moonlight.
Wouldn't you love to have me?
her sultry eyebrows imply.
I can show you the origin of man, nature, and beast.
Set you on fire with the passion of The Greats.
Lead you down blind alleyways and skip through the twinkling stars of
space.
Squeeze you close and ride the heartbeats of wild love.
Taste the salt lick of bottomless sorrow
and vibrate with the dulcet wind chimes of easy mirth.
I'll set your mind alight with vibrant images, resonant emotion, and
toppling magnitude.
I'll lead you to the precipice of greatness, take your hand, and jump.
You're in for the most glorious triumph or the most gasping loss of
your dreams.
Will you come with me, knowing I won't be with you all the time?
I'll never be there when you call, but when I come, in my own time,
you'll exist as if on fire.
A flash of light and the space she occupied is a void of stars, dead
leaves, and possibility.
The dazzling conundrum of the Blue Muse.

Twin Souls

The past made eye contact with me this morning,
As I looked up from scrambled eggs for a minute.
There stared the eyes of an ambitious young man
Alive, in a nook, on the dresser.
Dapper raven hair, in the 20s style
Cool grey eyes like hot flint
A strong full face in the prime of youth
Shaped exactly like my mother's
Delicate, finely contoured lips
Beautiful and still so masculine
Polished off by a small cleft in chin
It's the face of a man who never backs down,
Though the man's spent twenty years dead.
Those eyes are much different from those I remember,
I saw as Death took measurements for its veil.
But I wasn't afraid then, never afraid,
I was only a child, embarrassed.
"Should I see this? I'm so young, Mama,
And there's nothing I can do to stop it.
I wish Grandpa wasn't like this now.
There is silence here, where it shouldn't be silent."
I recall the sunken, pale, dead face
Sleeping in a cold casket bed
The eyes no more to see tiny me,
No longer to alight, with suffering and love
On the small innocent face
Of an imaginative daughter's child.
There he stares with a face I've never known,
Watching me as I start my day.

I can still see the spirit in those Kodak eyes,
And a chill runs over and through me.
That spirit I know very well,
I understand because it is mine too.
I will smile at him, blowing a kiss
When those black and white eyes meet mine.
And maybe I'll see his spirit in Heaven,
While a grandchild meets my photographed face.

Simple Romanticism

Who knew that soap
Could carry dreams
In bubbles of flirtation?
Close enough to touch,
They POP!
Swirly rainbow orbs
Of promises and teasing
Break against my skin
In delicate bubble kisses.
You gave me these bubbles
In a translucent bouquet,
Made by breath of affection.
Such an innocence!
Childlike purity.
The simple way to say
I love you.

Mermaid

Sea treasures of red kelp, shells, pearls braided and twisted into
her dolphin length raven hair, pinned up with purple urchin spikes

Metallic gold eyes sparkle like sun on the water, enchanting
And unsettling in contrast to small coral lips.
Bare moon white torso twisting, twirling through
The darkened water with graceful energy.
Her muscular tail of mother of pearl scales decorated with woven
chains of golden kelp.
Swimming alongside Narwhals, unicorns of the sea,
Uses giant scarlet jellyfish as an umbrella in shark storms.
Reads primitive sea god runes in her rainbow anemone garden,
Shared with stealthy Sea Dragons.
She sings sweeter than whales and dolphins,
Yet with the same haunted majesty of mysterious sonar.
She can breathe water and be exquisitely beautiful.
She is pure and free.

Oxford

Poetic city of spires
Tapestry of history
Rigid academia rules
Amidst unrivaled romance.
A world unto itself
Notice all it deems important
Little else comes into account.
It's a foreign dreamscape
Quickly familiar, like home,
Though you're clearly viewed "outsider"
If you try to believe in
Their special ways
The arrogance you detect
Will not matter.
To interact within it
Is to adoringly love it
It will claim all that it houses
Stay, if only for an hour
You are taken, a new possession.
It will purchase your spirit,
With those silent morning spires.
Polish and renovate you
Then, with noble indifference,
Watch you go back where you began.

Love Poem for a Ghost

You always wrote: "Come find me."
Then I promptly lost you.
I started my new life here,
You continued with your life there.
Is it strange we still run in the background?
I dissolve my wedding band mentality and slip into dreams.
You're another side of reality, which flashes in my mind:
We ran, hand in hand, by the Isis Canal
Faded into the eclipse, while I wore your fleece jacket.
Held hands in the magic of the meteor shower.
We were a warm summer rain in Christ Church Meadow,
Romeo and Juliet under the Bridge of Sighs
I made you my coat rack at the club,
Then chased you in the 2am alley to apologize.
Now we are a lifetime apart.
No longer the shy dreamers we once were.
What if Now and Then were the same strand?
If I could kiss you again, and it'd be all right.
You are my unfinished poem,
A fragmented melody without words,
Quietly humming underneath reality
A favorite half-remembered song from another time.

Raindrops and Mysticism

Pen nestled between my fingers
Notebook on my knee
Simon and Garfunkel
Above the raindrops
I gaze out my window
The world alive again
Like a photo with a green filter
And awakening from slumber
Melody of rain shower
mingles with splashing traffic,
vocal harmony and guitar,
dreams from my pen
I strum thoughts softly
tenderly stroke them into shape.
Measure fog in the forest, reflecting the sun.
My memories for others to disdain or treasure.

Dust

Violets
Symphonic
My heart backfires and rumbles
The bass line reverberates.
Insides twist and rise up
An ascension toward you.
Only you're not there...
I hear the snow fall
The splashing of traffic outside.
I am upstairs.
Alone.
And cold.
I skipped out on life today.
I sense its motion around me
Though right now I am still-
Still.........................still.......................
And searching.
Oh! Why this upheaval?
Why do my muscles trill
At each unnamed remembrance of you?
My mind tries to move on,
But my body persists in expectation
Longing to react to your energy, inches away
And feel the reality of attraction,
Instead of the memory.
Of a cold stone,
Grey light
An unreal existence
A synthetic breeze on crepe poppy petals
Ode to unending anticipation..................

Mama Miss America

I see the world around me get pulled into the whirling, wicked, game. Every day, every day more.

I see the future of America vomiting hot-dogs and apple pie at 5:04 in the morning with no one to hold back her hair and offer a Dixie cup of cold water to soothe the acid burned throat.

I see the comings and goings of the wretched and glorious belief holders and I remember it all. Every worthless movement. I note it.

I see those who look like eccentric feminist movement men. Who talk to you about the great women of the world and later say, "Woman, get back over here! Don't you turn your back when a man is talking to you!" Don't worry, Sugar, he was only kidding.

Who shelter the brain of a new millennium Einstein under the head of a purple haired punk. Writes Spanish love poems to the prettiest girl in the world and she laughs like a queen and says, "Have you ever read anything so stupid?"

Who lounge on the March 21st of their youth, taking laundry home to mama, two hours away. Reaching into daddy's pocket for a living allowance because it isn't fun to have a job.

Who spit blood over a dime library fine while the mother of four sticky children in her dirty turquoise jacket and worn out sweatpants pleasantly hands over a fifty for hers.

Who stare at their smartphones to dislike images of immigrant children in cages because it's fashionable to be outraged while you're scrolling the feed. Action is for someone else. Outrage is In. Action is so taxing.

Who chose as an elected representative of the people a man who plays naughty and keeps a toybox of synthetic women under the desk. Cares deeply for nothing more than himself, but it's okay. Everyone is also too busy being worried about themselves to do anything.

Who spit in the face of a homosexual, or a black man, or a refugee. I hear "Love thy neighbor" on their lips in the church and ugly slurs outside. Be loving to everyone around you, but destroy the ones you don't like.

Who abandon dreams of getting a Ph.D because there's no money in dreams. Conveniently, there's also no money for them.

Who write poems about the convulsing glory of the nation, shaking their heads in dismay, but can't think up a way to save it.

About the Author

S.J. Lomas is a cheerful Michigan girl who writes strange, and somewhat dark, young adult fiction. She loves books so much that she not only writes them, but she became a librarian and a book reviewer. Her to-be-read pile is large enough to last several lifetimes, but she wouldn't have it any other way. Keep up with S.J. on Goodreads, Facebook, Twitter, or her newsletter. If you've finished the book, please let other readers know what you thought by leaving a brief review on your favorite retailer site. Your time spent sharing your opinion is greatly appreciated!

Read more at www.sjlomas.com

www.ingramcontent.com/pod-product-compliance
Lightning Source LLC
Chambersburg PA
CBHW030011040426
42337CB00012BA/741